skate goals

SKATEBOARD PRACTICE JOURNAL

JUST SKATE
JOURNALS

THIS JOURNAL BELONGS TO

ADDRESS

PHONE

EMAIL

SOCIAL

SKILLS + TRICKS TO LEARN

EQUIPMENT WISH LIST

DATE

LOCATION

SESSION GOALS

NOTES

DATE

LOCATION

SESSION GOALS

NOTES

DATE

LOCATION

SESSION GOALS

NOTES

DATE

LOCATION

SESSION GOALS

NOTES

DATE

LOCATION

SESSION GOALS

NOTES

DATE

LOCATION

SESSION GOALS

NOTES

DATE

LOCATION

SESSION GOALS

NOTES

DATE

LOCATION

SESSION GOALS

NOTES

DATE

LOCATION

SESSION GOALS

NOTES

DATE

LOCATION

SESSION GOALS

NOTES

DATE

LOCATION

SESSION GOALS

NOTES

DATE

LOCATION

SESSION GOALS

NOTES

DATE

LOCATION

SESSION GOALS

NOTES

DATE

LOCATION

SESSION GOALS

NOTES

DATE

LOCATION

SESSION GOALS

NOTES

DATE

LOCATION

SESSION GOALS

NOTES

DATE

LOCATION

SESSION GOALS

NOTES

DATE

LOCATION

SESSION GOALS

NOTES

DATE

LOCATION

SESSION GOALS

NOTES

DATE

LOCATION

SESSION GOALS

NOTES

DATE

LOCATION

SESSION GOALS

NOTES

DATE

LOCATION

SESSION GOALS

NOTES

DATE

LOCATION

SESSION GOALS

NOTES

DATE

LOCATION

SESSION GOALS

NOTES

DATE

LOCATION

SESSION GOALS

NOTES

DATE

LOCATION

SESSION GOALS

NOTES

DATE

LOCATION

SESSION GOALS

NOTES

DATE

LOCATION

SESSION GOALS

NOTES

DATE

LOCATION

SESSION GOALS

NOTES

DATE

LOCATION

SESSION GOALS

NOTES

DATE

LOCATION

SESSION GOALS

NOTES

DATE

LOCATION

SESSION GOALS

NOTES

DATE

LOCATION

SESSION GOALS

NOTES

DATE

LOCATION

SESSION GOALS

NOTES

DATE

LOCATION

SESSION GOALS

NOTES

DATE

LOCATION

SESSION GOALS

NOTES

DATE

LOCATION

SESSION GOALS

NOTES

DATE

LOCATION

SESSION GOALS

NOTES

DATE

LOCATION

SESSION GOALS

NOTES

DATE

LOCATION

SESSION GOALS

NOTES

DATE

LOCATION

SESSION GOALS

NOTES

DATE

LOCATION

SESSION GOALS

NOTES

DATE

LOCATION

SESSION GOALS

NOTES

DATE

LOCATION

SESSION GOALS

NOTES

DATE

LOCATION

SESSION GOALS

NOTES

DATE

LOCATION

SESSION GOALS

NOTES

DATE

LOCATION

SESSION GOALS

NOTES

DATE

LOCATION

SESSION GOALS

NOTES

DATE

LOCATION

SESSION GOALS

NOTES

DATE

LOCATION

SESSION GOALS

NOTES

DATE

LOCATION

SESSION GOALS

NOTES

DATE

LOCATION

SESSION GOALS

NOTES

DATE

LOCATION

SESSION GOALS

NOTES

DATE

LOCATION

SESSION GOALS

NOTES

DATE

LOCATION

SESSION GOALS

NOTES

DATE

LOCATION

SESSION GOALS

NOTES

DATE

LOCATION

SESSION GOALS

NOTES

DATE

LOCATION

SESSION GOALS

NOTES

DATE

LOCATION

SESSION GOALS

NOTES

DATE

LOCATION

SESSION GOALS

NOTES

DATE

LOCATION

SESSION GOALS

NOTES

DATE

LOCATION

SESSION GOALS

NOTES

DATE

LOCATION

SESSION GOALS

NOTES

DATE

LOCATION

SESSION GOALS

NOTES

DATE

LOCATION

SESSION GOALS

NOTES

DATE

LOCATION

SESSION GOALS

NOTES

DATE

LOCATION

SESSION GOALS

NOTES

DATE

LOCATION

SESSION GOALS

NOTES

Made in the USA
Las Vegas, NV
13 November 2021

34333689R00079